the old bridge

Bellamy's Changing World: The River
was conceived, edited and designed
by Frances Lincoln Limited
Apollo Works, 5 Charlton Kings Road, London NW5 2SB

Text © 1988 by Botanical Enterprises Publications Ltd.
Illustrations © Jill Dow 1988

First published in Great Britain by
Macdonald and Co. (Publishers) Ltd,
Greater London House,
Hampstead Road,
London NW1 7RX
A BPCC plc Company

597.
6

British Library Cataloguing in Publication Data

Bellamy, David 1933–
The river — (Bellamy's Changing World: 2)
1. Stream ecology – Juvenile literature
I. Title   II. Dow, Jill   III. Series
574.5'26323   QH541.5.S7

ISBN 0-356-13570-5

Printed and bound in Italy

Design and Art Direction Debbie Mackinnon

Frances Lincoln Ltd. would like to thank
Pippa Rubinstein, Trish Burgess, Sarah Mitchell,
Kathy Henderson, Kathryn Cave, Stephen Pollock
and Jackie Westbrook for help with the series.

Bellamy's Changing World

The
River

David Bellamy

with illustrations by Jill Dow

Macdonald

This is a story about a river whose banks and water are home to many creatures. Lots of people enjoy it, too. It is a beautiful place, full of life and colour. Here it is in winter. Many birds have come to feed on the fruits of trees like the holly and hawthorn.

Ducks, mink and deer have left their tracks in the soft covering of snow at the icy river's edge.

Two ducks and a drake swim up to eat the crusts and grain that visitors have brought for them. A pike is looking for food, too. You won't see any frogs now: they stored their food away as a layer of fat in autumn before they hibernated and they are all fast asleep in the mud in the shallows.

It's early summer now. From the new concrete bridge you can look down into the clear dark water and see the giant pike lying in wait among the waterweed, beneath the storm overflow pipe from the food factory. The river is almost choked with water plants: rushes and sedges along the edge, and waterlilies and pondweeds nearer open water. A heron is standing looking for fish and frogs in the shallows. He has a nest in an old willow tree on the opposite bank from where a fisherman is casting his line.

Beside the river it is cool and damp. Swans and ducks swim up with their young, hoping to be fed. The air is buzzing with insects. The blue damsel-flies resting on the rushes spend much of their lives as rather ugly nymphs in the water. There they catch and eat other water insects, tadpoles and even tiny fish, before emerging to fly free.

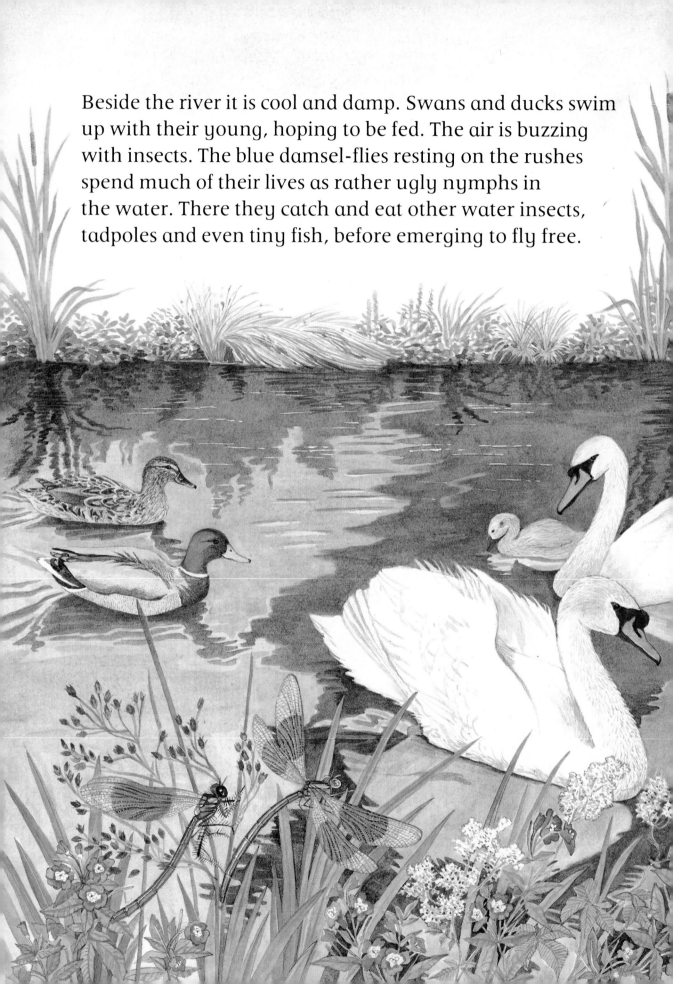

Scoop up some pond water in a shallow white bowl and see what you catch. Don't stand the bowl in the sun, because the creatures will get too hot, and put them back quickly. Here is a stickleback with a row of little spikes on its back for protection, a water boatman using its legs like oars, a pair of diving beetles and a long water stick insect.

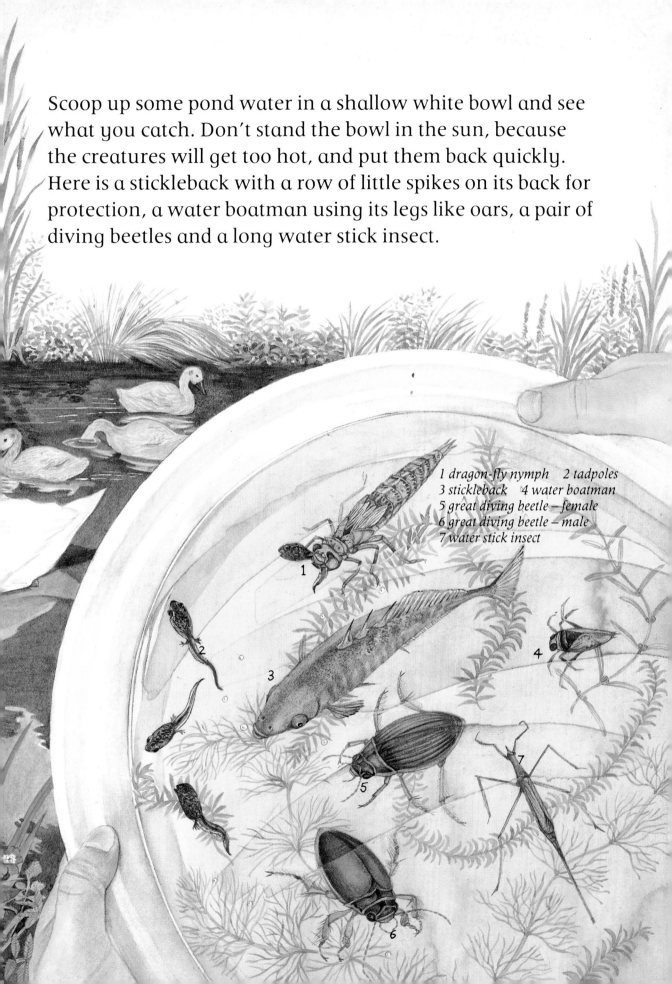

1 dragon-fly nymph   2 tadpoles
3 stickleback   4 water boatman
5 great diving beetle – female
6 great diving beetle – male
7 water stick insect

The young tench
in one of the
fisherman's long
nets are plant-
eaters, while the
carp eats plants and
worms. The eels in
the other net eat
fish and frogs.

The pike in this stretch of the river is so big it can eat all the other sorts of fish and even the ducklings. When the fisherman throws a handful of bait into the water to attract more fish, the drake flies in to enjoy a free meal. Good fishermen always leave the river clean and tidy, taking home any broken line, hooks and weights that might maim or kill birds and other animals.

1 water snail   2 snails' eggs   3 froglet
4 water scorpion   5 water boatman
6 freshwater shrimp   7 pond skater
8 water measurer

In the summer when it's hot and dry, the river flows very slowly. When the sun is shining, all the green plants crowding the river make oxygen that bubbles into the water. Some creatures – like the pike and freshwater shrimp – have gills which they use to 'breathe' the oxygen they need. The froglets have lungs and so must swim up for gulps of air, although when they were tadpoles they too had gills. The water boatman collects silver air bubbles on its hairy abdomen and the water scorpion takes in air through a snorkel-like tail.

Some insects, like the pond skater and water measurer, are so light they can walk or skim about on the surface of the water; small, flat, black worms and water snails can move along hanging down from the surface. The snails stick their eggs underneath the lily leaves where they won't dry up.

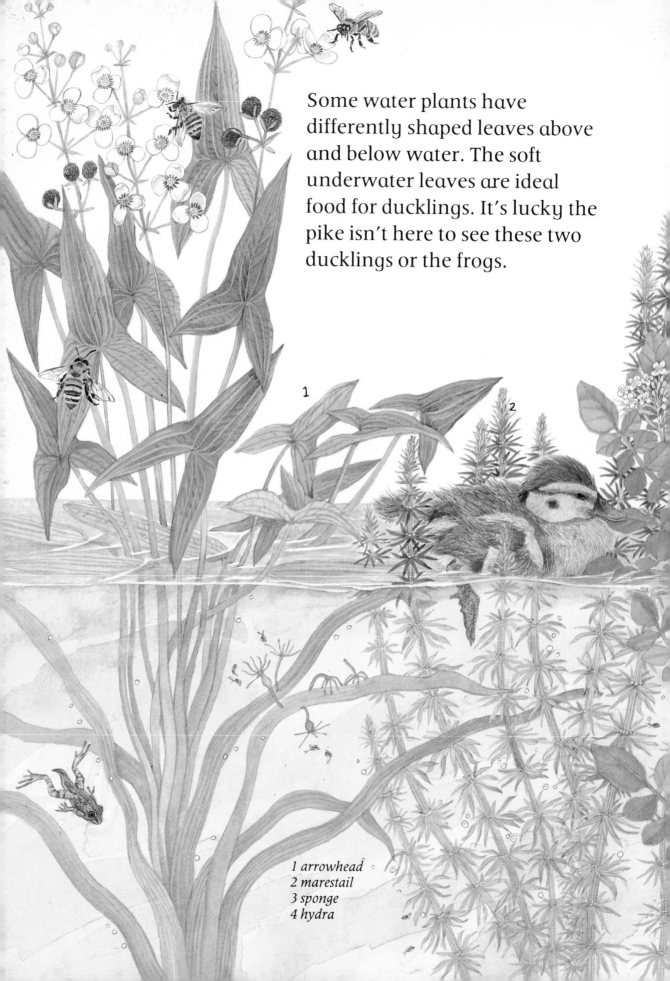

Some water plants have differently shaped leaves above and below water. The soft underwater leaves are ideal food for ducklings. It's lucky the pike isn't here to see these two ducklings or the frogs.

1 arrowhead
2 marestail
3 sponge
4 hydra

All sorts of creatures live on the old brick wall. A spider has caught a damsel-fly in its web and a mason wasp is laying her eggs in a crevice. Under the water, a sponge, which is a very simple animal, sieves food from the water, while green hydra somersault along on their tentacles and snails are eating watercress.

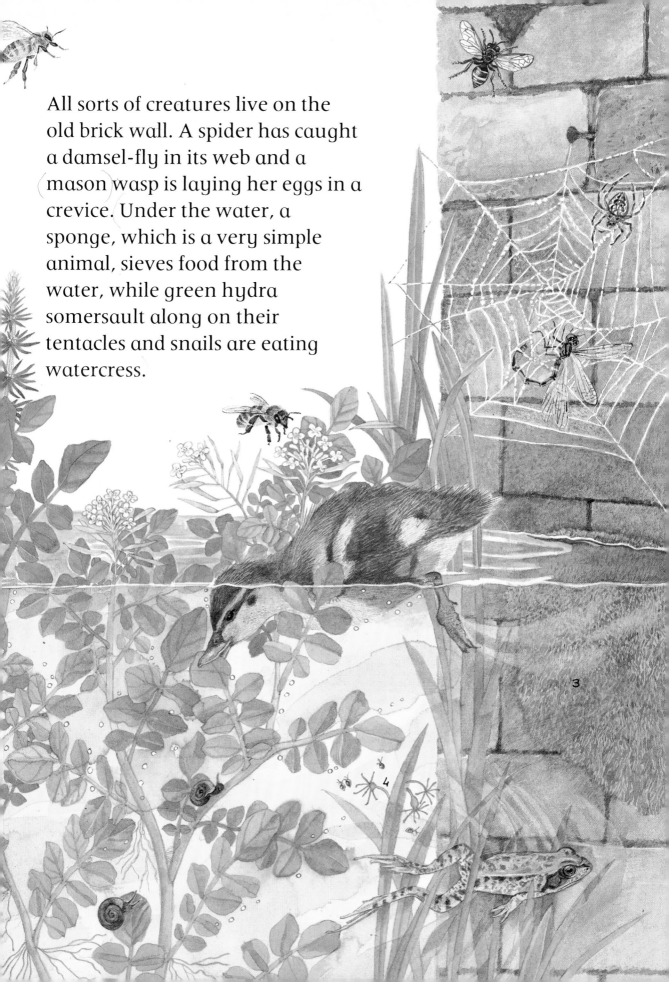

3

4

Here the river tumbles down an old weir and forms a riffle. Many creatures can live here because the falling water stirs in tiny bubbles of oxygen-rich air. The creatures have to hang on tightly, though, or they will get swept away.

1 may-fly   2 water-slater   3 dragon-fly
4 limpet   5 alder-fly larva   6 caddis-fly larva

The caddis-fly larvae protect themselves with houses made of sticks, leaves or tiny shells and stones. But when they turn into adult insects they, like the gnats and may-flies, are easy prey for the frog. The dragon-fly is out hunting the insects too.

3

The swallows swoop down to catch insects that have emerged from the water by the old stone bridge, and a water vole sticks its head out of a hole just above water level. Bees are buzzing round the Himalayan balsam, blue tits are collecting the soft covering of reed mace to line their nests, and a duck is calling one of her ducklings.

The old bridge is home to many living things. House martins have built their nests high up under the parapet and butterflies sun themselves on the stonework. The ice-cream man always stops here too. Some young visitors have crossed the bridge to buy cornets from him and tell him about all the interesting things they've seen on the river.

But back at the new bridge something terrible is happening. Filthy waste is pouring out of the factory pipe from the factory into the river. The fisherman has run off to sound the alarm.

The animals are getting away as fast as they can,
fleeing from the suffocating stream of waste, but the fish
and many of the small water creatures cannot escape.

rat-tailed maggot

The flow has stopped, but too late. The damage has been done. The water is covered with the bodies of dead fish, and the smell is terrible. Bacteria, too small to see, are at work breaking down the waste, but to do this they use up all the oxygen in the water. Without oxygen to breathe even the great pike and the eel can't survive. White sewage fungus, growing out of control in the polluted water, smothers the weeds. The only creatures that can thrive in the water are rat-tailed maggots, which breathe through a tail like a telescopic snorkel. The frogs are all right too, and sit on the bank feasting on the swarms of flies.

The black-headed gulls squabbling over their share of the dead fish are helping to clean up the mess.

Beyond the weir, at the riffle, things are better. The waste has been diluted, and the falling water stirs oxygen into the river, making it easier for river creatures to live. A small pike swims by and the mud between the stones is full of red bloodworms.

Tiny green plants called algae cover the rocks or trail in the water – they also bubble oxygen into the water and help make it clean again. The snails and ducks both like to eat algae. The frogs are catching clouds of mosquitoes and midges that have hatched out – you can see their empty pupae, as well as some larvae, hanging down from the surface of the water.

It is late summer now, almost a month since the disaster. The river is nearly back to normal and everyone who enjoys walking by the water or sitting on the bank hopes the factory owners will be more careful in future.

Under the old bridge, the river looks clean again. The water is a little greener from all the algae that are still growing, but sewage fungus no longer clogs the weeds. Frogs are croaking and bats are flitting around catching insects. The duck is sitting on a new nest among the reedmace. Although many fish have died, others have moved into this stretch, and the young pike is growing fast. Soon he will be the new king of the river.

the factory

the new bridge

the weir

the riffle